BEING A FO:

What it me

C000271837

A guide for young children

Written by Hedi Argent

BAAF
ADOPTION
& FOSTERING

Acknowledgements

I am grateful to Lorna Miles and her family for their helpful comments, to Karen Wilkins, Sam and Dan for their photographic skills, Chloe for artwork, and to Shaila Shah and Jo Francis at BAAF for their enduring patience and support. My most heartfelt thanks go to the foster families and the children they look after, who have taught me some of what they know.

Published by
British Association for Adoption & Fostering (BAAF)
Saffron House
6-10 Kirby Street
London EC1N 8TS
www.baaf.org.uk

Charity registration 275689 (England and Wales) and SC039337 (Scotland)
© Hedi Argent, 2011
Reprinted 2014

British Library Cataloguing in Publication Data
A catalogue record for this book is available from the British Library

ISBN 978 1 907585 40 1

Project management by Jo Francis, Publications Department, BAAF
Illustrations by Lynda Durrant unless otherwise credited
Photographs as credited; posed by models
Designed by Helen Joubert Design
Printed in Great Britain by the Lavenham Press

BAAF is the leading UK-wide membership organisation for all those concerned with adoption, fostering and child care issues.

If you are reading this book or having it read aloud to you, your family is probably going to foster, or perhaps you are fostering already like Max and his family.

Max is seven years old. He lives with his mum and little brother, Josh, who has just had his fourth birthday. They are a foster family.

Max is used to fostering now, but he had a lot of questions when his mum first saw the advert about becoming a foster carer.

This is a list of questions Max asked about fostering. You can tick the boxes after the questions you would like to ask.

What exactly is fostering? ☐

Is fostering different from adoption? ☐

Can anyone foster? ☐

Do foster families get paid? ☐

Why are we fostering? ☐

Why do children need foster families? ☐

Will they be my brothers and sisters? ☐

How long will the foster children stay? ☐

How many foster children will there be? ☐

Will I have to share everything? ☐

What if I don't like them or they don't like me? ☐

Where will they go when they leave? ☐

Will I see them again after they go? ☐

How can I help the children? ☐

Max's mum could answer some of his questions. The social worker, who came to talk to the family about fostering, answered all the rest. Max listened and learned some new words – these are written in red. **Social workers** find foster families and help them to look after the children they foster. Max liked the social worker, who was called Sam, because she talked about football as well as fostering.

© Karen Wilkins

Here are the answers to Max's questions.

◉ What exactly is fostering?

Children who can't live with the family they were born into need a foster family to look after them.

The word "fostering" means to care for, to nourish and help to grow.

All children need to grow up in a family that will care for them, **nourish** them and help them to grow. Families who foster are helping children to be healthy, happy and safe while they can't stay in their own homes.

At least forty thousand children in the UK are in foster care at any one time. Max thinks that's an awful lot of children. There are only two fostered children in his class at school, including his friend, Emmet. When all the class made **family trees**, their teacher explained that some children have two families: their **birth family** and their foster family. This is the family tree Max's friend, Emmet, made.

⊙ Some very famous people have been fostered

Samantha Morton, a British TV and film actress who has won several awards, lived with foster families and in residential homes from the age of seven.

Eddie Murphy, another famous actor, was fostered when his mother was ill.

Ice T, a famous rap artist who has his own record label, was fostered, and so was Kriss Akabusi MBE, an athlete who has won several Olympic medals.

Do you know any other famous people who were fostered?
Do you know anyone in your class or school who is fostered?
Do you know any stories about children who are fostered?

This story is about Tracy Beaker, who has lived in foster care. You can read the book or watch the TV series and film on DVD.

There are different kinds of fostering

Sometimes children are moved into a special foster family to stay for a long time. This is called **long-term** or **permanent foster care**. Max's auntie is a long-term foster carer. She has been looking after twin sisters, aged 13, since they were eight years old. They will stay with her until they are grown up because everyone has agreed it is best for them and they want to stay.

Disabled children who need a lot of special care may also sometimes need a short break away from home. Some families offer **short break foster care** for a week, a day or maybe just for a few hours.

Most often, foster families look after a child or children for a few weeks or months while their parents and social workers make plans for the future. This is called **short-term foster care**. Max's mum is a short-term foster carer. She has looked after 23 children! Seventeen of them went back home and six went on to be adopted.

⊙ Is fostering different from adoption?

If children can't go back to their parents, their social worker will find them a new family that will always be their family, even when they are adults. This means that they will usually be adopted. Sometimes foster families adopt a child they have been looking after.

It is easiest to think of adoption as a permanent, **legal** arrangement with new parents, and fostering as the best way to look after children while their home situation is being sorted out. Adoption is one way of building a family, giving birth is another. Both are good ways of having a family. Fostering is a way of caring for other people's children.

⊙ Can anyone foster?

All sorts of people can be foster carers. They can be a foster mum and dad or just a foster mum or just a foster dad; there can even be two foster mums or two foster dads. Some foster families, like yours, have children of their own and some don't.

This picture is made up of photos of different sorts of foster families. Can you pick them out?

Families who want to foster have to prove they are good at looking after children. And they must have enough room in their home for children to come and stay. A social worker visits people who want to foster to make sure they will be good carers. The social worker writes a report for a special meeting called a **fostering panel**. This panel decides whether families will make good foster carers or not, and tells the social workers.

Do foster families get paid?

Foster carers get some money from the council so that they can pay for extra clothes and food and outings and holidays for the foster child. This is called a **fostering allowance**. It means that foster carers can afford to look after foster children even if they don't earn a lot of money.

Max's mum had to buy a special seat and a buggy for the last baby they fostered. Max and his little brother went to the shop with Mum to choose toys for the baby. They wanted to buy everything they saw, but Mum said there was only enough fostering allowance to buy a couple of toys and they could each choose one. Max and Josh both wanted to buy the baby a teddy, so in the end they got two!

© Karen Wilkins

◉ Why are we fostering?

Families who foster want to look after children when they have to live away from their own homes. Perhaps they know a neighbour or friend who fosters and they see how important it is to look after these children. Sometimes there is a notice in a newspaper or a poster on a bus saying that there are children who need a foster family.

Have you or your mum or dad ever seen a notice or poster like that?

Max's family has always fostered. His grandma fostered when his mum and his auntie were little girls, his auntie fosters now and his mum started fostering when Max was five. Max's mum sometimes fosters babies who are going to be adopted. Max loves babies. He is sad when they go, but he is always glad when he knows they are going to have a new family of their own. This is a picture Max painted of himself, his mum and little brother waving goodbye to baby Jade with her new parents.

© Chloe Ashdown

Why do children need foster families?

If a child is not happy at home or not properly looked after, a teacher, or neighbour, or family member or friend may tell the council. Sometimes a child's parents may ask the council for help. The parents may be ill, or they can't manage, or have nowhere suitable to live, or they may be afraid that their child will get hurt. A very few children may not have parents.

Children can ask for help themselves if they are having a bad time at home. They may speak to a teacher, a neighbour, a social worker, or telephone **ChildLine**.

In every case, social workers will visit the child's home and may move the child away to make sure she or he is kept safe and well. The social workers then have to go to **court** to tell the child's story to a **judge**, who can make an **order** for the child to be looked after by the council. This usually means that the child will need a foster family.

Will they be my brothers and sisters?

The children you foster will be like brothers and sisters while they are staying with you because they will be treated like every other child in the family. If they stay quite a long time, it will feel like having a brother or sister. If they stay for a very short time, it will feel more like having a visitor.

But foster children also have their own families, and that usually includes their own brothers and sisters.

Perhaps it is best to think of all the children you foster as your "foster brothers and sisters". That will help everyone to understand how and why children come and go in your family. But you may have to explain to your friends what fostering means.

Max calls all the babies they foster his "foster babies". He gets his mum to take photos of each one so that he will remember them all. Sometimes they look at them together.

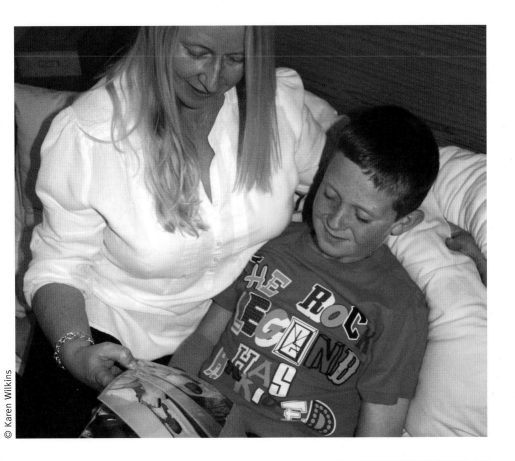

© Karen Wilkins

◉ Do foster children see their own families?

Sometimes parents and other relatives come to visit foster children in their foster families. Sometimes foster children meet up with their families at a place they all know, like a **Family Centre**. Sometimes the children can visit their parents and brothers and sisters at home. Some foster children may see their own families very often and others not very often.

Social workers say that children who keep in touch with their families are having **contact**. It is good for most children to have contact with their families, but for a few it is not possible or the child may not want it.

When children have to leave their own homes, it is best for brothers and sisters to stay together in the same foster family. If they have to be separated, it is important for them to keep in touch. Getting together can be fun for the foster children and their foster families.

Max says that he sometimes feels a bit left out when the foster children's parents visit and bring presents or treats for their children, but Max's mum usually notices and finds a special treat for him and for his little brother, Josh.

What do you think are the treats Max and Josh like best?

TICKET

⊙ How long will the foster children stay?

Most foster children will stay as long as it takes social workers to sort out whether they can go home to their own families or whether they need a new permanent family. Some foster children will stay for only a few weeks and others for a few months. Some foster children who can't go back to their own families may stay with the same foster family for a long time or even until they are grown up.

Sometimes, if children come in an **emergency**, they may come without much warning and only stay for a few days. But usually there will be **introductions** so the foster children and the foster families can get to know each other before they live together.

Max had a special book where his mum helped him to write down the dates when their foster children came, and how long each one of them stayed.

How many foster children will there be?

That depends:
- on how much room you have in your house;
- on how many children are already in the family;
- on how much time foster families can spend with their children; and
- on the arrangements foster carers make with their social workers.

Some foster families take only one foster child at a time. Other families may take two or even three children. Whenever possible, sisters and brothers will be **placed** together in the same foster family, like the twins with Max's auntie.

Max and Josh never have more than one foster brother or sister because they live in a small house and their mum says she has enough to do looking after the two of them and one more!

 # Will I have to share everything?

Children who live together don't have to share everything. If you have favourite toys or things that are precious and you are afraid they might get broken, you can ask your mum or dad to find you a special place to keep them safe. Max has a collection of football trophies he has won that he keeps on a shelf in the sitting room.

Do you have any special toys or other things you don't want to share? Where would you like to keep them?

All children sometimes fight and argue about who can play with what or who had it first! And all parents sometimes get cross when their children bicker – especially if they make too much noise.

Some foster children may not know how to play or share because they have never had toys of their own and nobody has played with them. They hold on tight to all their belongings because they are afraid someone will take them away. By sharing your toys, you can help them to see that it's more fun that way.

The most important thing you will have to share is your parents' time. That's just like sharing your parents with any other brothers and sisters except that foster children won't stay for ever like the brothers and sisters born in your family. Sometimes you may think that the foster children are getting more than their fair share of attention. That could be because they have had too little attention in the past and are trying to make up for it.

 ## What if I don't like them or they don't like me?

You can't like everybody, no one can.
There may be times when you get fed up with one of the foster children, and it's OK to feel like that. You don't have to pretend that you are happy when you are not. It will make you feel better if you talk about it with your mum or dad.

If children have been treated unkindly, it may take quite a long time for them to stop being angry and unkind themselves. They may be confused and homesick and scared and that could make them behave quite badly.

Foster care can teach children who have been hurt that families can be kind and safe. You are an important member of the foster family and foster children will learn from you how to behave better and how to make friends.

Try to imagine what it must be like to have to leave your home and family and to live in a strange house with strange people, to sleep in a bed that is not like your bed at home, and to eat food you're not used to.

How do you think you would feel?
Can you draw a face to show how you would feel?
What could foster children learn from you?

 # Where will they go when they leave?

Most foster children go back to their own homes and their own parents. Sometimes they go to live with grandparents, other relatives or family friends: this is called **kinship care**. If they can't go back to their own families, they may move to another family to be adopted or to a permanent foster family. Not very often, foster children go to live in **boarding schools** or **residential homes**.

Will I see them again after they go?

It's always sad to say goodbye to people you've grown fond of, and foster families have to say a lot of goodbyes. You will miss some foster brothers and sisters a lot, especially if they have stayed a long time and you have got on really well. But there may be some foster children you won't miss at all because you didn't get on together, or they didn't stay long enough for you to grow used to them. In any case, your parents will know where they have gone, and whether you can visit each other or meet up.

Sometimes social workers decide that it is best for foster children to settle into their new homes without looking back. Sometimes families want to make a fresh start and forget the past.

But it is never good to lose friends, and it is always best to make arrangements to keep in touch when foster children leave. Letters, emails and phone calls, as well as seeing each other, are ways of keeping in touch.

Max puts photos of all their foster children in his album, so that he can remember them even if they don't keep in touch.

You might like to start a photo album of all the children you foster. And you could write, or ask a grown-up to write something you would like to remember about each of them.

How can I help the children?

When your family fosters, you are part of the fostering team, but you are not responsible for the foster children – your parents are.

Social workers will ask you how you feel about fostering and listen to what you have to say.

Your parents will talk to you about the children who come and go.

These are some important things you can do when you foster:

- Make the foster children feel welcome – think what would make you feel welcome in a strange home.
- Help them to know how your parents want children in your house to behave. They may not understand the rules in your family or not be used to keeping to rules that make them safe.
- Introduce them to your friends and neighbours.
- Show them how to play and share.
- Give them time to settle down and don't expect too much of them too soon.
- Be ready to help your parents a bit more when there is extra work to be done.

And finally...

If you have other questions that Max did not think of, you should ask your mum or dad or one of the social workers. If you have any worries about fostering, it really is OK to let the grown-ups know.

You are an important member of your fostering family and what you think and feel matters.

Fostering is an important job and we hope that, like Max, you can make new friends, have fun and help children in need.

Words that may be new to you

Social workers are trained to look after children and families who need help. They make sure that foster children are well looked after and that foster families get all the support they need.

To **nourish** means to give food and love to help children grow.

Family trees are drawings that show who is in your family and how they are related to each other.

The **birth family** is the family you are born into.

Long-term or **permanent foster care** means that children usually stay for a long time or until they are grown up.

Short break foster care is for children, including disabled children, who need a lot of care and short holidays away from home.

A **legal** arrangement is one that agrees with laws that say how things should be done.

Short-term foster care is the most usual form of care for children who need to live with another family when they cannot stay in their own home.

A **fostering panel** is a group of people who know about fostering and recommend whether families should look after other people's children.

A **fostering allowance** is paid to foster carers for all the extra expenses when they foster.

ChildLine is a special 24-hour helpline for children who are in trouble or in danger of being hurt. Tel: 0800 1111.

Court is the place where decisions are made about children who need to be fostered.

A **judge** is a woman or a man who makes decisions in court.

Orders are the decisions a judge makes.